D0131161

DISCARD

MIGHTY MILITARY MACHINES

Military Rifles

Fierce Firepower

Gerry Souter

Enslow Publishers, Inc.
40 Industrial Road
Box 398
Berkeley Heights, NJ 07922
USA

http://www.enslow.com

Library of Congress Cataloging-in-Publication Data

Souter, Gerry.
  Military rifles: fierce firepower / By Gerry Souter.
      p. cm. — (Mighty military machines)
  Includes bibliographical references and index.
  ISBN 0-7660-2662-0
  1. Rifles—United States—Juvenile literature. I. Title. II. Series.
  UD390.S68 2006
  623.4'425—dc22

                                        2006009219

Printed in the United States of America

10 9 8 7 6 5 4 3 2 1

To Our Readers:
We have done our best to make sure all Internet Addresses in this book were active and appropriate when we went to press. However, the author and the publisher have no control over and assume no liability for the material available on those Internet sites or on other Web sites they may link to. Any comments or suggestions can be sent by e-mail to comments@enslow.com or to the address on the back cover.

Photo Credits: 2006 by Colt Defense LLC, used with permission, all rights reserved, p. 9; Department of Defense, pp. 1, 6, 7, 16, 22, 24, 25, 27, 30, 43, 46, 47; Getty Images, pp. 4, 14, 18; Library of Congress, pp. 3, 13; North Wind Picture Archives, p. 12; North Wind Picture Archives/Nancy Carter, p. 10; U.S. Army, p. 21; U.S. Marine Corps, pp. 3, 29, 32, 33, 34–35, 36, 37, 38, 40, 45.

Cover Photos: Department of Defense

Contents

Chapter ONE

Alone in the Dark

The night of January 23, 2002, was moonless and dark. Master Sergeant Anthony Pryor of the 5th Special Forces Group in Afghanistan could see only with his night vision goggles. His patrol was attacking buildings occupied by opposing soldiers. Because there were women and children in the village, bombs could not be dropped from planes. This was a foot soldier's job. Gunfire suddenly blasted from windows and soon the air was alive with the hum of passing bullets.

Pryor rushed into a building at the head of his squad. Two Afghan soldiers appeared in a doorway. He and his men fired first with their M4 rifles.

Sergeant Pryor went through the door alone as his men returned fire from outside. In the dark room, three opposing soldiers were firing out windows at American troops. The men at the windows were green shapes in Pryor's goggles as he fired his rifle again and put them out of action.

As he reloaded his M4, Pryor was struck from behind by another Afghan soldier and knocked down. His goggles were ripped off as he fought hand-to-hand with the soldier on the floor. Across the room, the other three had only been wounded and were groping for their weapons in the dark. Pryor rolled away from the soldier who had attacked him. He then lunged for the spot where he had dropped his rifle. When he found it he swung the barrel toward the soldiers. The room exploded with gunfire. Rifle flashes lit up the walls. In a few seconds, Pryor was the only soldier still alive in the darkness.

For thinking of the safety of others in his special forces group before his own that night, Master Sergeant Anthony Pryor was awarded the Silver Star. This is a medal given for gallantry in action.

The Modern Combat Rifle

The U.S. military counts on the firepower and strength of the modern combat rifle. This rifle, the M4, was introduced to the Marines in 2002. It has become the standard weapon of the Army and

Marine Corps. It is a shorter, lighter, and more practical version of the M16, a military rifle used around the world. The M16 was a huge step forward in military rifle design when it was introduced in the United States in the 1960s. It is the perfect example of how rifles have been improved over the years to keep up with new technology. The M4 is the latest in a long line of military rifles that have constantly been improved to help make U.S. soldiers the best in the world.

FACTFILE

Rifles vs. Guns

In the military, the word "gun" is not used to refer to a rifle. A "rifle" is a firearm with a rifled, or grooved, barrel, such as the M4. The word "gun" refers to a cannon-type weapon. The large M-119 Howitzer, shown here, is a gun that is commonly used by the Army today.

▲ A shell casing flies from an M4 rifle after it is fired by a U.S. soldier. The soldier was taking part in a firing exercise.

Winning battles has often required soldiers on foot to occupy the opposing force's ground. These soldiers need weapons that can defeat that opposing force in both close fighting and from some distance away. For a military rifle like the M4 to do these jobs, it must have several features:

1. It must be rugged and able to withstand mud, water, explosions, and being dropped.

2. It must be reliable and able to shoot on a target over long and short distances, called ranges, of twenty-five to three hundred meters, whenever a soldier picks it up.

3. It must shoot powerfully over long distances and must be able to fire a bullet that will stop opposing soldiers. The bullet must shatter against hard surfaces so it does not bounce and injure innocent civilians (nonmilitary people).

4. The military rifle must be light enough to carry and easy to use for many different jobs. These include fighting over long distances in the desert, up-close in rooms and hallways in buildings, in cities, and where trails are narrow between thick bushes and trees.

Every American soldier must accept the tremendous responsibility that goes with carrying a deadly weapon. From the American Revolution to

FACTFILE

Millimeters, Inches, and Calibers

Military ammunition is always named after its diameter in millimeters. For example, a 7.62 millimeter (mm) bullet is 7.62mm in diameter. Outside of the military, the term "caliber" refers to a similar measurement, but in inches. A 7.62mm bullet is about .30 inches in diameter, or .30 caliber. In other words, a 7.62mm military bullet is the same as a .30-caliber civilian bullet.

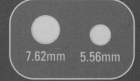
7.62mm   5.56mm

The inside of the rifle's muzzle is also measured in millimeters. Rifle barrels are made to accept bullets of one size only, based on the width of the muzzle. The 5.56mm M16 rifle, for example, can fire only 5.56mm bullets.

FACTFILE

Parts of a Rifle

The modern military rifle has six basic parts:

1. The **stock** supports the rifle against the soldier's shoulder.

2. The **action** is a collection of mechanical parts that make the rifle shoot.

3. The **trigger** connects the finger of the shooter to the mechanism that fires the rifle. Squeezing the trigger with the finger releases the firing pin that fires the ammunition in the rear of the barrel.

4. The **barrel** helps guide the bullets toward the target. The front end of the barrel is called the **muzzle**. The rear of the barrel is called the **breech**.

5. The **sights** help the soldier aim the barrel at the target.

6. The **magazine** holds the rifle's ammunition.

the present, American soldiers have fought to protect peoples' rights and liberties. Many soldiers have given their lives in battle so others could be free. The one weapon every soldier must master to win these battles is the military rifle.

Chapter TWO

The Evolution of the Military Rifle

The earliest hand-carried gun was no more than a smooth tube containing a lead ball and gunpowder held at arm's length. To make the gun shoot, the shooter touched a burning match to a hole at the rear of the barrel. This ignited the gunpowder at the back of the tube, and the lead ball exploded from the barrel's muzzle.

By the late 1700s, frontiersmen, trappers, and hunters were using hunting rifles made in Kentucky and Pennsylvania. Instead of a smooth tube for a barrel, these weapons had spiral grooves called "rifling" carved into the inside of their barrels. The grooves dug into the fired bullet as it passed down the barrel. This caused the lead ball, or bullet, to spin as it left the rifle. The spinning made the bullet go straighter and more accurately to a distant target. Rifling was a new invention that had come from Europe.

In the Revolutionary War (1775–1783), American colonial soldiers used these accurate hunting rifles against their British opponents. They were able to shoot from a distance and stay hidden. British officers fell from their horses not knowing from where the Americans' shots had come. But soon the British were using men called "snipers" armed with their own accurate rifles against the Americans.

After the Civil War (1861–1865), all combat weapons had rifling in their barrels. Some were

FACTFILE

What Is a Sniper?

The first "snipers" were men in medieval England who hunted a small, delicate bird called the snipe. The dainty birds were cooked and eaten in meat pies. Specially trained men hid in trees, sometimes under cloaks covered with leaves and twigs. They waited quietly near the birds' nests. These "snipers" then quickly caught the birds with a net.

Riflemen who hid and waited quietly for a target to appear during a battle also eventually became known as snipers, after the bird hunters.

loaded from the rear or breech instead of from the muzzle. These "breechloader" rifles used brass or copper cases called cartridges (or rounds). Inside the cartridge was a bullet and the propellant, or gunpowder, that would ignite and explode, forcing the bullet down the barrel and out the end of the rifle. Using cartridges, more shots could be fired faster.

▲ Using their accurate hunting rifles, American soldiers were able to act as snipers during the Revolutionary War.

The First Modern Combat Rifle

Gun designers worked through the following decades to make rifles even more efficient. In 1936 the first semi-automatic military rifle was invented by John Garand. Military rifles before that time fired one shot at a time and the cartridges, also called rounds, were reloaded by hand. Garand's weapon, called the M1, could fire eight preloaded cartridges, one at a time with each pull of the trigger. American soldiers in World War II

(1939–1945) were the only soldiers to have these semi-automatic rifles.

"Semi-automatic" means the rifle could fire multiple shots before reloading, but the trigger had to be pulled once for each shot fired. "Automatic" means that as long as the trigger is held down, the weapon fires until all the ammunition in the magazine is gone.

Later, during the Korean (1950–1953) and Vietnam (1959–1975) Wars, it became clear that

A U.S. soldier in World War II aims his M1 Garand rifle. The ▼ M1 was the first semi-automatic rifle used in combat.

▲ A soldier tracks through the jungle with his M16 rifle during the Vietnam War. Later models of the M16 had special features that were developed to withstand Vietnam's jungle warfare and harsh conditions.

American soldiers would need an automatic weapon—one that was lighter in weight and more rugged. A new military rifle had to be developed.

The U.S. Army wanted their new weapon to have high accuracy for single shots as well as automatic fire. A rifle that had been designed by Eugene Stoner in 1956 fit the bill. It was a stunning change from standard rifles made of wood and steel. Stoner used aluminum for the casing that housed the operating parts and trigger, called the receiver. Also, the shoulder stock was made of plastic. This resulted in a rifle that weighed only seven pounds (the M1 weighed more than nine pounds). The rifle also had a built-in carry handle which contained the sights used to aim the shot at a target.

The Army had found its new weapon. The M16, as it came to be known, was a very important development in military rifles.

FACTFILE

Metrics and the Military

The U.S. military measures everything using the metric system. This is because the metric system is used throughout the world, and is a system that all countries recognize. So instead of inches, yards, and miles, the military uses millimeters, meters, and kilometers (also called "klicks").

1 millimeter = about .04 inch (a tiny fraction of an inch)
1 centimeter (or 10 millimeters) = about .4 inch (just under half an inch)
1 meter = about 3.3 feet, or 1.1 yard
1 kilometer (or 1000 meters) = about .6 mile (just over half a mile)
1 kilogram = about 2.2 pounds

Using the metric system, a football field, which is 100 yards long, is about 91.4 meters. A 100-pound person weighs about 45.4 kilograms.

Chapter THREE

The M16

Major Colin Risso of the British Army was traveling in a convoy, or group of vehicles, made up of both British and American troops in Bagram, Afghanistan, in 2004. As the vehicles drove down into a narrow, dry streambed called a wadi, bullets suddenly rained down on them from all sides. Rocket-propelled grenades (RPGs) slammed into the trucks and showered the soldiers with fire and sharp splinters. Amid the smoke and flames, Major Risso grabbed the nearest rifle, an M16. He quickly began to return fire.

Bullets and grenades crashed into the stalled vehicles from all sides, but Major Risso saw that most of the firing was coming from the right bank of the wadi. He also saw that some of his own troops were in trouble because their grenade launcher had jammed. Risso grabbed another rifle, an M4, and fired a heavy blast of constant gunfire with the two rifles. Ducking his streams of bullets, the opposing side was unable to shoot back. By the time

Major Risso fired a heavy blast of constant gunfire with the two rifles.

the convoy commander was able to get the vehicles moving again, Risso had fired more than 150 rounds of ammunition.

Using American weapons, Major Risso had helped the Americans and British fight their way out of the ambush. The good design of the M16 he had picked up made it a simple, reliable weapon to use. It helped make his actions successful. For those brave actions, Major Colin Risso was awarded the British Military Cross.

Improving the M16

In 1962, the U.S. Army adopted the first version of the M16 (called the M16A1) and it became the standard weapon for soldiers heading to Vietnam beginning in 1965. Soldiers using today's updated M16 have a better rifle because of the lessons learned the hard way with the M16A1.

Military Rifles: Fierce Firepower

In Vietnam, rain, mud, sweat, and grit got into the M16A1 rifles and gummed up their working parts. The rifles had to be taken apart and cleaned with a special kit that every soldier carried. Also, the breech into which the cartridges were fed from the magazine became rusty. Empty cartridge cases jammed in the breech and had to be pried out with a knife. Many soldiers were killed or wounded because their rifles jammed during a fight, and they could not defend themselves.

▼ A U.S. Marine is helped up by another Marine as they wade through a marsh in Vietnam in 1967. Soldiers' M16A1 rifles suffered great damage from these wet, muddy conditions.

FACTFILE

The General's Dessert

Gobs of red pulp flew into the air as the bullet struck. Another shot banged from the rifle and a second splash of red stained the grass. The general lowered his smoking weapon and squinted at the third target. "We'll eat that last watermelon for dessert," he said. In July 1960, Robert MacDonald of Colt Industries, who wanted to manufacture the new rifle invented by Eugene Stoner, invited Air Force General Curtis LeMay to a birthday party. LeMay was asked to try the rifle. Three watermelons were set up outside at different ranges as targets. LeMay fired twice and exploded two of the melons, saving the third for dessert.

Back in Washington, General LeMay told Secretary of Defense Robert S. McNamara about the new rifle. LeMay ordered 8,500 of the rifles for Air Force police units. Soon, after more design changes, the new weapon became the famous M16.

American rifle designers worked on the problems as fast as they were reported. The rusted breeches were plated with chrome to stop rust. New stronger, long-lasting magazines to hold ammunition were assembled. A muzzle "brake" was added to the front of the barrel. This brake kept the muzzle from rising every time the rifle fired by blowing gas from each shot upward. By keeping the rifle steady, the brake allowed a soldier to keep the sights on the target.

FACT FILE

Who Produced the M16?

When the M16 was first issued to American soldiers, they were used to a heavier rifle with a wooden stock and steel moving parts. Soldiers thought the lightweight aluminum M16 with its plastic stock seemed more like a toy. In the 1960s, the toy company Mattell actually did produce the "Marauder," a toy M16 that looked liked the real thing. This helped fuel a myth that the real M16 was also made by the toy company, but Colt Manufacturing was the maker of the real M16.

Full automatic fire was replaced by three-shot bursts of fire with each trigger pull. This saved ammunition and still allowed firepower when needed in close quarters or facing crowds of attacking enemy soldiers.

It was very hard to see the opposing forces in the dim jungle light or near dawn and twilight. A special "light gathering" sight was designed for the M16 that made the scene seem brighter under dim conditions so soldiers could more easily see their targets.

For additional firepower an M203 grenade launcher could be attached beneath the barrel of the M16A1. This launcher acts like a small cannon that fires a 40mm explosive, tear gas, or smoke grenade. The 15-inch tube can be attached in the field or can remain on the M16 rifle adding only three pounds to the rifle's weight. The M203 grenade launcher gives soldiers a powerful weapon against lightly armored trucks, machine guns, heavy doors, or when firing into buildings to stop opposing fire.

As the improvements arrived on the battlefield, soldiers became more confident with their rifles. The changes resulted in a second version of the M16 called the M16A2, introduced in the early 1980s. The M16A2 became the standard rifle of the Army and Marine Corps until the M4 rifle replaced it in 2003. The basic design of the M16 has gone on to become the longest serving rifle in U.S. military history.

A U.S. soldier in Samarra, Iraq, prepares to return opposing ▼ fire. He is armed with an M4 rifle with an M203 grenade launcher attached underneath.

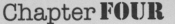

Chapter FOUR

The M4 and the Future of Combat Rifles

Kevin Donell Vance was an eight-year Air Force veteran with the rank of staff sergeant. He was aboard a Chinook helicopter that was forced down by opposing fire in Afghanistan on March 4, 2002. Vance's helicopter was on a rescue mission to bring back an American soldier who had fallen from another helicopter during an earlier mission. Vance was near the helicopter's back door when opposing ground fire suddenly slammed into his chopper, sending it into a turning, twisting spiral. The

Chinook, along with its twenty-one crew members, crashed to the ground.

Many of the crew members including the pilot were injured, and Vance was the only uninjured man on board with combat training. He quickly directed the crew members who could still shoot to defend the chopper, while he tried to contact his base to get help. Afghan soldiers fired from a nearby building. Their bullets thudded against the downed helicopter's metal skin and dug furrows

Opposing ground fire suddenly slammed into the chopper, sending it into a turning, twisting spiral.

in the dusty soil around it. The chopper's windows shattered. The smell of fuel and hot oil was heavy in the air.

"I was shooting an M4. At first, I had to keep firing at the enemy, to hold them back and then to find help for CAS [close air support] on the radio," Vance wrote later.

While Vance's wounded crewmen tried to communicate with their base, he was under constant enemy automatic weapon fire. "First, we shot M203 rounds at a bunker," Vance wrote. "An M203 is a grenade launcher that fits on a M4/16. As the squad leader and team leader shot M203s, I stood up and provided covering fire. When he would

▲ U.S. soldiers pour from the back of a Chinook helicopter. They had arrived near Samarra, Iraq, to clear the area of opposing soldiers.

stand up to fire a grenade at the bunker, I would stand up and shoot at the bunker to cover him. I did the same when the crew members would run for more ammo [ammunition]."

Vance fought for thirteen hours until air strikes by F-15 fighter planes and reinforcements arrived. The rescue mission had turned into a full-scale

Insurgent Weapons

American soldiers often have to fight against terrorists and insurgents, or fighters who rebel against authority. These fighters get their weapons from many sources around the world. In the Middle East, many insurgents use the AK-47 Kalishnikov rifle. It is an assault rifle that was created in Russia following World War II. The AK-47 is one of the best military rifles ever designed. It is durable, easy to shoot, and inexpensive to build.

Insurgents also often use rocket-propelled grenade (RPG) launchers. The grenade is a missile with fins to guide it. The special explosive inside the grenade can destroy lightly armored vehicles, sandbag protection, and most building construction.

Insurgents and terrorists also make their own weapons. Improvised Explosive Devices (IEDs), for example, are buried near roads. They are set off with remote-control radio signals or cell phones when a vehicle passes by.

Other homemade bombs are packed with scraps of metal,

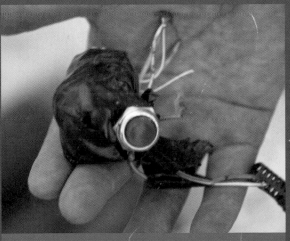

A homemade push-button trigger for an IED.

nails, and tiny steel balls. When they explode, the small, sharp objects are forcefully sent in every direction. These homemade bombs are extremely dangerous.

battle. Covering gunfire finally allowed Chinook helicopters to land and rescue the fifteen survivors.

"I went through so many different emotions: excited, mad, frustrated, sad, any other emotion you could possibly feel," Vance wrote after the fight.

The M4

The M4 rifle, a shorter version of the M16, was originally requested by the U.S. Marine Corps in 1983 as part of a Modular Weapons System (MWS) program. The Marines wanted a version of the M16 that could be used as a Close Quarters Battle (CQB) weapon. The M16 design had to be shortened by trimming back the barrel and making the stock

FACTFILE

The M4A1 Rifle

The new M4A1 rifles are very adaptable to many combat situations. The carry handle rear sight that is a feature on all M16s and M4s can be removed. A flat cover called a Picatinny Rail can then be installed. The Army calls this the Rail Interface System (RIS), which allows a variety of attachments, such as sights, lasers, flashlights, and other devices to be added to the rifle.

Some sights available for the M4A1 use a laser pointer. A laser pointer is a tiny projector that shows a red mark on the target at the point where the bullet will strike. Other sighting devices allow a soldier to see targets at night. The M4A1 is becoming the standard-issue military rifle for American soldiers.

The smaller M4A1 rifle is useful in Iraq since much of the ▲
fighting is done in cities instead of open battlefields. This
soldier is patrolling the city of Mosul.

collapsible. The new rifle was only twenty-six inches
long compared to the almost forty-inch-long M16.

The M4 was given to tank crews who needed
shorter weapons to carry in their tanks' cramped
spaces. The latest version of the M4, the M4A1, is
now being given to troops fighting the war in Iraq

because much of the fighting takes place in cities and villages instead of wide-open spaces. Patrols moving through narrow streets carry the M4A1 rifle to stop ambushes and clear out opposing snipers.

The Future of Military Rifles

Since the American Revolutionary War, the U.S. military has tried to build better and better weapons using the latest technology available.

FACTFILE

Air-Burst Ammunition

Future military rifles will feature air-burst ammunition. This ammunition allows soldiers to fire standard 5.56mm bullets and 25mm rounds that can explode in the air above a target, scattering sharp metal fragments.

Engineers and scientists at the U.S. Army's Picatinny Arsenal weapons research and development center in New Jersey are constantly working to do this. These new and better weapons will improve the effectiveness and combat survival of all military personnel.

According to Picatinny designers, the military rifle of the future will have air burst or grenade launch capability, advanced electronic sighting, and will be able to shoot further. Their goal is to put these improved weapons into the hands of every soldier as soon as possible.

Just as the lighter and shorter M4 replaced many M16s, the new weapons being designed now will be even more lightweight. These new weapons will lighten the soldier's load, reducing exhaustion over long marches. This will allow soldiers to complete their missions more easily and successfully.

The Army is now considering three rifles that meet the latest requirements: the XM8, the XM25, and the

A Marine officer demonstrates ▲ the features of the XM8 assault rifle. The XM8 is one type of rifle being developed that may replace the M16 and M4.

Mark16/17. Any of these rifles can give American soldiers an advantage in combat. Some are being tested in the field by Special Operations forces. As they have for centuries, U.S. soldiers in the future will be able to defend themselves and the freedom of others with the best weapons in the world.

Chapter FIVE

Today's Sniper Rifles

In the spring of 2003, a group of American soldiers gathered on a nearly moonless night before an attack on a water treatment plant in Samawah, Iraq. High above the city, seated on a walkway around the top of a water tower, an American sniper peered across the rooftops. The telescopic sight mounted on his Barrett M82 13mm rifle magnified his vision by ten times. In the dim light, he saw a movement almost a mile away. The movement was an opposing soldier crossing a rooftop carrying an RPG launcher on his back. The sniper watched as the distant soldier moved toward a place where he could ambush the American soldiers.

The sniper aimed carefully, slowed his breathing, and blinked his eyes to clear his vision. He slowly squeezed the rifle's trigger and fired across a distance of about 1,400 meters. The bullet took a full two seconds to travel from the rifle's muzzle to the target.

On the distant rooftop, the opposing soldier fell, probably never hearing the sound of the rifle's shot. During the Americans' attack the next day, there would be one less opposing soldier firing RPGs. The American sniper's single shot may have saved many lives.

Snipers in the Military

American snipers were first used effectively during the Revolutionary War. They used the first rifles that could hit a target at a range of about 275 meters using a long rifled barrel. But the military thought these sharpshooting soldiers were "murderers" and "assassins" who hunted their targets from trees and from behind fences. Armies at that time and also during the Civil War usually stood and faced each other, firing their rifles as a group on command.

▲ A U.S. Marine sergeant uses a tripod to stabilize his M24 sniper rifle during sniper training in Japan in 2004.

► The scope of a sniper rifle clearly shows a target hundreds of meters away.

Snipers were very effective, and all armies used them. Even so, at the end of every war all sniper training stopped because commanders considered the extra training unnecessary and too expensive.

Today, both the Army and Marine Corps have permanent sniper training schools and use snipers in warfare. American snipers are trained to defeat opposing snipers. They hit individual targets at great distances, forcing the other side to stay undercover.

Snipers can also knock out opposing vehicles from as far away as 1,500 meters with the largest rifle used in today's combat. Their shooting skills have saved many American and civilian lives.

The Army M24 Sniper Rifle

In 1986, the U.S. Army held trials to find out what manufacturer made the best rifle for use as a sniper weapon. The award went to the Remington Arms Company for a version of their popular hunting rifle. With many changes, it became the M24 sniper rifle.

A single shot "bolt action" was designed for the rifle. This action loads a new, full cartridge from the magazine into the breech after each shot. The trigger, heavy barrel, and very powerful telescopic sight of the M24 are designed based on the rifles used in the shooting contests of the Olympic Games. With the telescopic sight, a distant target can be seen clearly. It also allows a marksman to make very fine adjustments so the shot will be as accurate as possible.

For combat use in jungle mud, desert sand, and rocky areas, every part is made stronger. The

FACTFILE

Bigger Rifle, Longer Range

In the 1980s, Ronald Barrett designed a ten-shot semi-automatic weapon that used a large 13mm cartridge. Today, these Barrett M82A1 and M99 Heavy Sniper weapons are used in Iraq and Afghanistan as long-range rifles that can knock out lightly armored equipment, cars, or trucks from 1,500 meters to 3,000 meters.

The M82A1 is large and heavy. It weighs 33.8 pounds and is 57 inches—almost five feet—long. Two legs extend beneath the rifle's muzzle to help support its weight. A target a mile away is no longer out of range.

On the end of this M82A1 (above) is an attachment that decreases the rifle's recoil and also hides the flash produced by the rifle as it fires. This helps the sniper to stay hidden.

FACTFILE

The Ultimate Rifle Test

Every year at Camp Perry, Ohio, rifle competitions are held. These competitions test the finest U.S. military and civilian marksmen and -women. The National Trophy Team Match is one event in the competition. It is nicknamed the "Rattle Battle" because of the large amount of ammunition fired in a short period of time.

In the Rattle Battle, teams must shoot at eight targets while firing from a prone, or lying down, position at six hundred yards and five hundred yards. (The Rattle Battle is a civilian-sponsored event, so U.S. measurements are used instead of metric measurements.) When the teams move to the three hundred-yard line, they must shoot from a sitting position. If they have any ammunition left, they fire the remaining rounds in a standing position at two hundred yards. At each stage, they have fifty seconds to fire as many accurate shots as they can. Above, members of the Marine Corps Rifle Team fire their rifles from the prone position.

In 2005, the U.S. Marine Corps won the Rattle Battle over the heavily favored U.S. Army team.

weather-proof shoulder stock is custom fitted to each sniper so the rifle can be held rock steady on a target. The M24 rifle weighs twelve pounds. Snipers must be in top physical shape to carry both their rifle and their full field equipment every day.

The Marine Corps M40 Sniper Rifle

In 1966, the U.S. Marines were already using the Remington Olympic-quality target rifle as their model M40 sniper weapon. In the 1970s, the Marines added a stronger plastic stock and a better telescopic sight. The M40 was now the M40A1, but by the 1990s, the Marines wanted to design a new rifle from scratch.

The result was the M40A3 sniper rifle. This model used the same bolt action as the Army M24 rifle. The Marines added a shoulder stock that can be adjusted in the field.

A Marine sniper looks ▶ through the scope of his M40A3 rifle.

Chapter SIX

Military Rifle Training

A military rifle is only as good as the soldier who uses it. Shooting skills often mean the difference between life and death in combat. When they enter the military, even the most experienced civilian hunters and target shooters have to learn the mechanics of combat shooting if they are going to survive or be able to support their fellow soldiers. All of the military services offer marksmanship training for all of their recruits, or those new to the service. The Army and Marine Corps stress good rifle handling, because that is their primary job.

Rifle training has changed as the role of ground troops has changed. Skills learned on a rifle range become life-saving reflexes in combat. Mastering the combat rifle also builds self-confidence in civilian life.

Today's average combat soldier must fire on targets as close as twenty-five meters and as far away as three hundred meters. Full automatic fire is often needed at close quarters in addition to controlled single-shot shooting at distant targets. Quick decisions must be made. Only through training are those decisions turned into instant reflexes under the stress of combat.

Soldiers learn to quickly set their rifle sights on targets at various distances. They also learn how to handle their weapons safely when not fighting. Today's rifle training teaches soldiers how to recognize targets on city streets and inside buildings. Under the stress of combat, it is often difficult to tell innocent civilians from dangerous opponents.

Military Recruit Marksmanship Training

Army and Marine training teaches recruits the basics of marksmanship with their service rifle. Both services use similar training techniques. This training takes place over two weeks, the first of which is called Snap-In Week. During this week, recruits practice shooting from four positions (standing, kneeling, sitting, and prone, or lying down). A Primary Marksmanship Instructor shows recruits how to fire, how to adjust their sights, how to take into account the effects of the weather, and other shooting skills. Recruits also have the chance to fire on the Indoor Simulated Marksmanship Training (ISMT) machine.

At an ISMT range, trainees fire laser-fitted weapons at simulated targets that are projected onto large screens. There are also "shoot/no-shoot"

▼ During Snap-In Week, recruits learn to fire their rifles from four different positions. These recruits wait for the order to approach the line and begin shooting.

FACTFILE

Rifle Qualification

Every soldier must qualify as an infantry rifleman on the training rifle range with an M16 or M4. To qualify means that a soldier must fire a certain number of shots at targets set up at different ranges. The rifle must be fired from different positions, too: prone, kneeling, sitting, and standing.

Each target is marked so the soldier receives a certain number of points, depending on where the target is hit. A center hit gets five points. A hit near the edge of the target gets only one point. The soldier must get a minimum number of points to qualify at each range. The higher the number of points, the higher the qualification the soldier receives from "marksman" to "sharpshooter" to the highest, "expert."

By the time the soldier receives the final qualification, the soldier and his or her rifle are a team. This teamwork is important, because the soldier's life often depends on it.

exercises, where a simulated enemy is shown standing next to a simulated innocent civilian. It helps soldiers know how to recognize and react to such situations.

During the second week of marksmanship training, recruits actually fire rifles on a course at ranges of 75, 175, and 300 meters. Recruits prepare for a test, or rifle qualification, on Friday of that week.

When this basic rifle training is complete, Field Firing Range (FFR) training begins. FFR is devoted to firing weapons in more realistic conditions. During earlier marksmanship training, recruits learn how to fire at a single target from one location. During FFR, recruits learn how to fire at moving and multiple targets, while under low-light

FACTFILE

Lining up the Sights

Every military rifle has a front and a rear sight. During training, a recruit is taught how to combine, or align these two sights and then place this "sight picture" on the target. When the front sight is positioned in the hole of the rear sight, this "alignment" is placed over the target to make the sight picture.

Then the trigger is squeezed until the rifle fires. Soldiers learn that it is important to slowly squeeze the trigger, not jerk or yank it. Jerking or yanking the trigger moves the sight alignment off the target, spoiling the sight picture at the instant of firing. Jerking the trigger also moves the barrel away from the target, and the bullet will miss.

rear sight
(closest to soldier)

front sight
(located further
down the barrel)

target

A soldier adjusts another soldier's field protective mask ▲ during an exercise. Soldiers must learn to handle their rifles while wearing the masks, which are difficult to see through.

conditions and wearing their field protective (gas) mask. This mask is designed to protect the soldier in the field from breathing harmful gases used as weapons. The mask covers the soldier's face. The soldier sees out through two clear plastic lenses and breathes through an air filter. It is difficult to see to the left or the right. It can be hot and sweaty inside the mask. The recruit must learn to fire without being able to wipe his or her eyes. Recruits are trained to shoot while peering through this dusty plastic with poor vision to the sides—a difficult task.

To graduate from marksmanship training, a recruit must score at a certain level in order to earn one of three designations: Marksman, Sharpshooter, or Expert Rifleman. The highest award, an Expert Rifleman designation, can be the first step to becoming a sniper. The higher the designation a soldier earns, the better the opportunity for advancement in rank. Soldiers can request to take the test again to try to improve their score if necessary.

Carrying a rifle is a badge of honor with a long tradition of courage and pride.

A soldier in rifle training develops skills such as self-discipline, physical control of muscle groups, eye-hand coordination, and responsibility for handling a deadly weapon in a safe manner at all times. Learning the rules of safe rifle handling and taking responsibility for the safety of those nearby is an important life skill. Soldiers learn that carrying a rifle is a badge of honor with a long tradition of courage and pride. These qualities translate into any civilian career path once a soldier's military career has ended.

Driving a car, using power tools, or mastering a difficult sports technique all require practice and learning each step to reach a goal. Rifle training is even more demanding. Once a bullet leaves the barrel it can travel over a mile and injure someone the shooter cannot even see. Rifle marksmen always know where their weapon is pointed. They always make sure that their weapon is safe when not actually pointed at a target. They know they hold the lives of other people in their hands.

For a U.S. soldier or Marine, successful training is part of their duty to themselves, their unit, and their country.

FACT FILE

What Is Marksmanship?

Just as they do today, early rifle users practiced their shooting by trying to hit targets, or marks, placed at a distance. A mark might have been an apple on a post, a v-shaped notch cut into tree bark, or a circle drawn on a piece of paper. A shooter who could hit close to the center of the mark became known as a "marksman." "Marksmanship" is the ability to shoot accurately at a target. Both terms are used in today's military to describe soldiers trained in using their rifles.

action—The collection of mechanical parts that makes a rifle shoot.

barrel—The tube down which a bullet travels out of a rifle.

bolt—A sliding block that seals the rear of a rifle when the rifle fires. The bolt slides to the rear, removing the empty cartridge case, and is then slid forward to feed a fresh cartridge from the rifle's magazine into the breech.

breech—The rear of a rifle's barrel, where ammunition is loaded to be fired.

cartridge—A small case that contains a rifle's ammunition and propellant. Also called a round.

civilian—A person who is not a professional soldier.

grenade—A small bomb that can be thrown by hand or fired from a launcher.

magazine—A box loaded with ammunition that fits into a rifle.

marksmanship—The ability to hit a target with a shot from a certain distance.

muzzle—The front end of a rifle barrel.

night vision—A system of battery-powered goggles, binoculars, or rifle sights that increase a soldier's ability to see at night by electronically magnifying the available light.

range—The distance from one point to another.

sight—A hole on a rifle that a shooter looks through to aim the rifle at a target.

stock—The part of a rifle that is held against a shooter's shoulder and cheek.

trigger—The part of a rifle that is squeezed to start the action of the rifle's firing.

Books

Blohm, Craig E. *Weapons of War.* San Diego: Lucent Books, 2003.

Hogg, Ian V. and John S. Weeks. *Military Small Arms of the 20th Century.* Iola, Wis.: Krause Publications, 2000.

Jones, Richard D. *Jane's Infantry Weapons 2005–2006.* Surrey, England: Jane's Information Group, 2005.

Long, Duncan. *The Complete AR-15/M16 Sourcebook: What Every Shooter Needs to Know.* Boulder, Colo.: Paladin Press, 2002.

Walter, John. *Military Rifles of Two World Wars.* London: Greenhill Books, 2003.

Internet Addresses

http://www.pica.army.mil/PicatinnyPublic/products_services/ products08.asp
  The U.S. Army's Picatinny Arsenal describes the various rifles they develop

http://www.usmilitary.about.com/od/armyweapons/l/ aainfantry1.htm
  An overview of military weapons, including the M16A2 and the M24 sniper rifle

http://www.globalsecurity.org/military/systems/ground/
  A page with a large index of military firearms, including the XM8 and XM25

INDEX